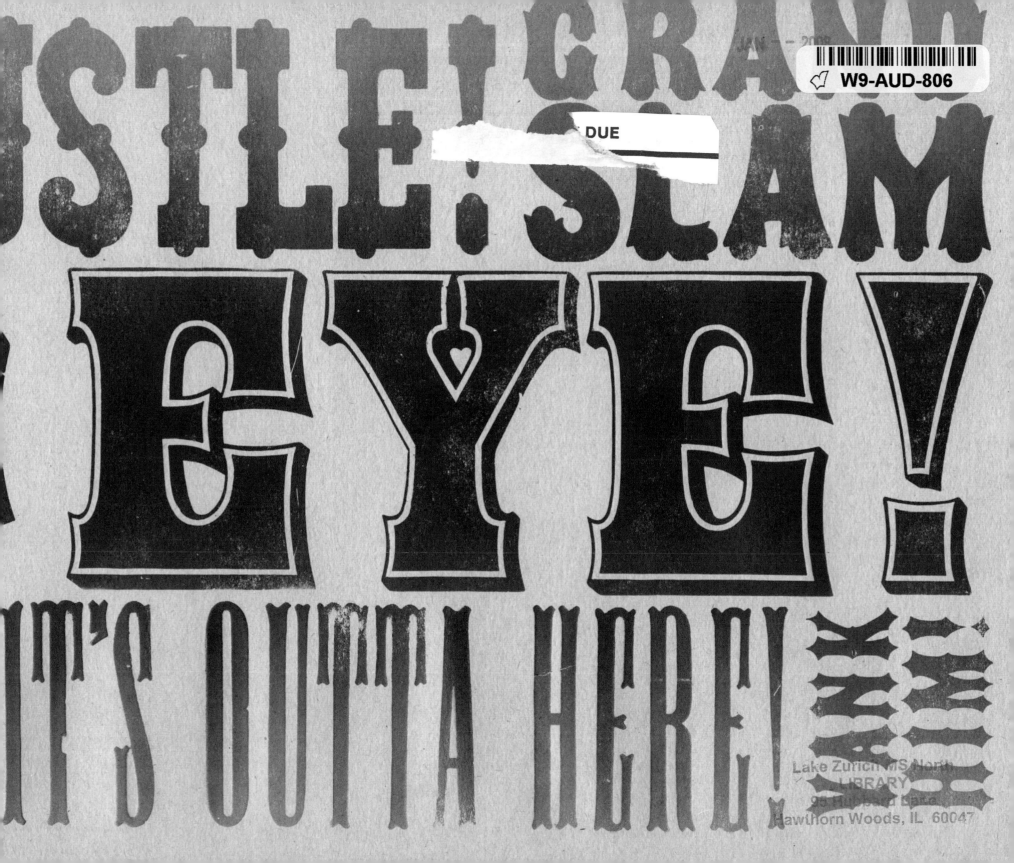

HEY BATTA BATTA SWING!

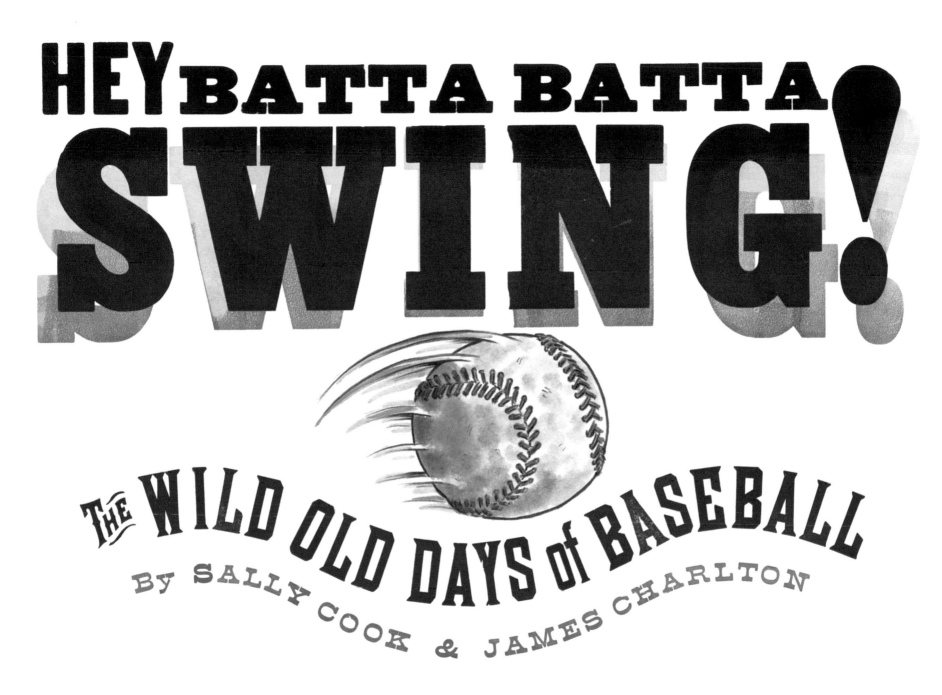

THE WILD OLD DAYS of BASEBALL

By SALLY COOK & JAMES CHARLTON

ILLUSTRATED by
ROSS MacDONALD

MARGARET K. McELDERRY BOOKS   New York London Toronto Sydney

Margaret K. McElderry Books

An imprint of Simon & Schuster Children's Publishing Division

1230 Avenue of the Americas, New York, New York 10020

Book design by Debra Sfetsios

The text for this book is set in Rockwell.

The illustrations for this book are rendered in watercolor

and pencil crayon, with some letterpress wood type.

Printed in the United States of America

10 9 8 7 6 5 4 3 2

Library of Congress Cataloging-in-Publication Data

Cook, Sally.

Hey batta batta swing! : the wild old days of baseball /

Sally Cook and James Charlton ;

illustrated by Ross MacDonald.—1st ed.

p. cm.

ISBN-13: 978-1-4169-1207-1 (hardcover 13 : alk. paper)

ISBN-10: 1-4169-1207-X (hardcover 10 : alk. paper)

1. Baseball—United States—History—Juvenile literature.

I. Charlton, James, 1939–. II. MacDonald, Ross. III. Title.

GV867.5.C653 2007

796.3570973—dc22

2006008132

For Luke Davoren—S. C.

For Harry, Sam, Tyler, and Sarah—J. C.

For Big J and Tiny D—R. M.

Three cheers to our teammates Holly McGhee,

Michael Steiner, Mark Fowler, Shecky Blackett,

Emma Dryden, Karen Wojtyla, and Debra Sfetsios;

heavy hitters Alex Cook, James and Sam Williams,

Jack Gilpin, Robert Stropp, Ben Green, and

Scott Flatow; and our awesome families.

W

HAT WAS THE GAME
OF BASEBALL LIKE
IN EARLIER TIMES?

Was it easier? Probably not! Different? You bet! More than a

hundred years ago baseball was just getting started, and the

rules were nothing like they are today. Sure, baseball was played

on a diamond with three bases and a home plate, but that's

where the similarities end. In the beginning, before there were professional teams, you could get a runner out by **soaking** him.

Ouch! It's no wonder that this practice only lasted a few years.

Almost every aspect of baseball, from the rules of the game to

the names of the teams, has changed over the years.

soaking: a very early rule that allowed a runner who was off base to be put out by hitting him with a ball

Team Colors

Just take a look at uniforms. You might think that every player—short, tall, **banjo hitter**, and **ace**—has always worn the same uniform as the rest of his teammates. Not so in 1882! That year owners decided that the players had to wear colored jerseys showing the position they played, *not* the team they played for.

banjo hitter: a poor hitter

ace: the team's best pitcher. One theory of its origin is that the word is short for Asa Brainard, an ace pitcher of the 1860s and 1870s.

Each player wore a cap, belt, and stockings of the same color, with white pants and a white tie. How confusing it must have been for the fans, or **cranks**, to see what one player called a "bed of tulips" on the field!

Even the players themselves were often baffled by the colors. A sportswriter was watching one game where a first baseman was the runner, so both the runner and the infielder right next to him were dressed exactly alike. The pitcher, Old Hoss

Radbourn, now in the Hall of Fame, threw over to first base to try and pick the runner off. But he threw to the wrong player, not to his teammate. Old Hoss was disgusted with the error, which he blamed on the uniforms.

The jerseys weren't popular with the players. "We may as well be wearing clown costumes," one complained. About mid-season, the team owners agreed with the players. By 1883 owners ruled that each team could choose its own uniform except for the stockings, whose colors would be decided by the leagues.

The teams in Boston and Chicago wore socks whose colors became the teams' nicknames—the Red Stockings and the White Stockings (now the Red Sox and the White Sox). Players from the defunct Troy (New York) Haymakers were signed by John Day, owner of the newly formed New York Giants, but they kept the green stockings, so the team was sometimes called the New York Green Stockings. Long before the Giants moved from New York to San Francisco in 1958, they discarded their green stockings for black ones.

Though the uniforms became different colors, they were all made out of heavy wool flannel, something you might wear in the wintertime. Can you imagine playing baseball in the hot sun wearing winter clothes?

In the 1880s fielders didn't wear gloves. Imagine a **fly chaser** playing bare-handed: no problem if the hit was a **can of corn**, but catching a **frozen rope** without a mitt? *Ow!* You can bet there were lots of **gappers** and **tweeners**. By the 1890s almost all the players were using leather mitts that looked like winter gloves, with a couple of strands of leather between the forefinger and thumb. Sometimes players cut off the gloves' fingers to get a better grip on the ball. In 1889 major league catcher Harry Decker was granted the first patent for a padded

fly chaser:

an outfielder

can of corn:

an easy fly ball

gappers:

hits between

outfielders

tweeners:

hits between

infielders

frozen rope:

a hard-hit line drive

13

catcher's mitt. It became so popular that for several years catcher's mitts were referred to as "deckers." By the early twentieth century, baseball gloves had evolved into a smaller version of what you see worn by players today.

Playing with Numbers

Maybe you think that **fans** were always able to identify their favorite players by number. Well, think again! In the early 1880s it was scorecard sellers who wanted the teams to put numbers on the players' uniforms. The Reds did just that in 1883: Numbers were sewn right on the sleeves. "Now we look like convicts!" many of the players said. At first, fans were confused and thought that the players were being ranked by their ability. Nobody understood this system, and it was soon dropped. It wasn't until 1929 that the idea was revived again, when the New York Yankees and the Cleveland Indians became the first teams to permanently stitch numbers on the backs of

their uniforms. The first hitter in the lineup was assigned number 1,
the second got number 2, and so on. For the Yankees, Babe Ruth, who
batted third, received number 3; the cleanup hitter, Lou Gehrig,
got number 4.

fans: One theory is that the word is shortened from "fanatics."

The term "Murderers' Row" is most commonly used to describe the 1927 Yankees. The heart of their lineup featured future Hall of Famers such as Babe Ruth and Lou Gehrig.

Within a few years all the teams had put numbers on their uniforms, and they were no longer assigned by batting order. Eventually players' last names were added to their uniforms as well. In the 1960s one team put a player's birthday on the back of his uniform! How did this happen? The player Carlos May, who wore number 17, was born on May 17. So his uniform read "MAY 17." One player even had his hometown on the back of his uniform: He wore number 96 because he was from Ninety-Six, South Carolina.

Players have always had

favorite numbers. Catcher Sandy Alomar Jr. wore his beloved number 15 for eleven seasons in Cleveland before he was traded to the White Sox. His number was being worn by Sox rookie catcher Josh Paul, who gave the number 15 to Alomar for a new set of golf clubs. That's the same price that Hall of Famer Don Sutton paid for his number 20 when he signed with the Oakland Athletics in 1985. The cost was a bit higher when Roger Clemens signed with the Blue Jays and Carlos Delgado gladly gave him number 21. Clemens showed his appreciation by giving Delgado a watch worth more than $15,000. But not every player cares what number he wears. Pitcher Walt Masterson, for example, played eleven seasons with the Washington Senators and wore seven different numbers.

Playing Catch

By the time teams put numbers on their jerseys, uniforms were provided by the team. But this wasn't always so. As late as 1910,

tools of ignorance: catcher's equipment

players had to pay about thirty dollars for their uniforms, which included one for home games and a different one for road games. Players had to pay extra for their bats, mitts, and equipment. Imagine what catchers had to pay for their **tools of ignorance**!

Today the catcher wears the most equipment of any player, and he did way back then as well. Fred Thayer patented the first catcher's mask in 1877, after he had a local tinsmith make one for him. Catchers started wearing the mask after a rule change that allowed them to make a **putout** on a bounce of a ball that had been tipped foul. Since the catchers stood so close to the batters, without masks they were in danger of chipping their teeth, or worse.

putout: When a fielder tags a base runner out, catches a fly ball, or catches a thrown ball and touches a base to make a force out, he gets credit for a "putout."

Chest protectors followed soon after, and by the early 1900s, catchers started wearing shin guards, too. Other changes, like wearing a throat guard and the modern batting helmet, didn't happen until after 1960.

The umpires behind the plate thought the masks were such

STRRRRIKE!

arbiter: another name
for an umpire. They were
also called "Men in Blue,"
because they used to wear
blue woolen uniforms.

a good idea that they, too, started wearing them. Then they began wearing shin guards and chest protectors. Bill Klem, a legendary **arbiter** in the National League, wore his chest protector under his jacket, claiming that he could see the pitches better that way.

Soon all the National League umpires wore their protectors under their jackets. When the American League became a major league in 1901, all the umpires in that league wore their chest protectors on the outside, and they continued to do so for most of the twentieth century. So the National League umpires had their style, and the American League umpires had theirs. Umpires had to buy their own equipment back then, and they still do today.

Name That Team

Some players in Cleveland may not have been too happy about shelling money out for their uniforms. In the 1890s Cleveland's team was called the Spiders, and players had to wear jerseys with a large spiderweb on them. If wearing such a uniform was supposed to "bug" the opposing team, it didn't work. In 1899 the Spiders had the worst season in history. They won only 20 games and lost 134—still the worst record today!

In 1901 the Spiders were gone from Cleveland and their new team was the Blues. Maybe that wasn't a popular color among fans, because the next year they changed their name again, this time to the Naps, after their star player-manager, Napoleon Lajoie. Talk about a fickle team! In 1915 they changed their name yet again to the Indians, supposedly after Lou Sockalexis, a former player and Penobscot Indian. But rumor had it that the owner simply liked the name, and that is how they are still known.

Another team, the Dodgers, first played in Brooklyn, New York. In the 1880s many of the fans

24

traveled to their games by trolley car. To get across the busy Brooklyn streets, people also had to dodge the trolleys, so the fans were called the "Trolley Dodgers." In 1889 the team became the "Bridegrooms" because so many of its players got married over the winter. That name didn't last long, and after a while the team went back to being the Dodgers. There aren't many trolley cars today, but the Dodgers are still around—even though the team has been in Los Angeles since 1958.

In 1891 the Pittsburgh Pirates were known as the Alleghenies. Then they signed Lou Bierbauer, a player who had broken his contract and left the Philadelphia Athletics. Why did he leave? To make more money! The Athletics were furious when their player didn't return and called the Pittsburgh team "piratical." The team has been known as the Pittsburgh Pirates ever since.

senior circuit:

the National League. The American League, which came later, is known as the junior circuit.

swipes:

steals of bases

Wouldn't you think with a name like the Pirates that they would top the **senior circuit** in **swipes** each year? They often have!

Name That Player

It wasn't just the teams that had nicknames, of course. The players did too. Frank Baker became known as "Home Run" Baker after he hit two homers in the 1911 World Series. He didn't even hit 100 in his entire career. Dizzy Dean earned his nickname when he was a minor league pitcher. He struck out so many batters in one game that the opposing manager said to his players, "Are you going to let that dizzy kid make a fool out of you?"

Larry Berra was named Yogi by a childhood friend, who thought he looked like a yogi. George Herman Ruth Jr. was nicknamed "the Babe" when a player saw Baltimore Orioles manager Jack Dunn with his new player and said, "There goes Dunnie with his new babe." Gabby Harnett was given the nickname by his Cubs teammates when he was a rookie. He was very shy and didn't talk or "gab" much. Negro League great Satchel Paige got his nickname when he was a boy because he invented a gadget for carrying more than one satchel, or piece of luggage, from the train station to earn money. There are several versions of how another Negro League star, "Cool Papa" Bell, got his nickname, but everyone agreed he was lightning fast as a runner. One story went that Cool Papa could turn off a bedroom light switch, jump into bed, and be under the covers before the room turned dark.

By some accounts, pitchers "Catfish" Hunter and "Blue Moon" Odom were given their nicknames by Oakland Athletics owner Charlie Finley, who thought all players should have nicknames. Over the years there have been several players named Rhodes, so naturally their teammates named them "Dusty." That's better than "Pickles,"

patrolled the pasture:

played in the outfield

which was William Dillhoefer's nickname. Some nicknames are given in admiration by opponents. Pitcher Walter Johnson was called "the Big Train." Pete Rose was "Charlie Hustle" because he was always trying harder. He would even run to first base after he was walked. Stan "the Man" Musial was given his nickname by Dodgers fans after he led the Cardinals to a series sweep against the Brooklyn team. Bob Ferguson, who **patrolled the pasture** for different teams in the nineteenth century, caught every ball he could reach. A teammate proclaimed that Bob was "Death to Flying Things." He was also called "Fighting Bob." Now, how do you suppose he earned *that* nickname?

Tricks of the Trade

Back when baseball first started, stealing bases was common, and so was a little cheating. There was only one umpire for each game, compared to the four umpires used in today's games. So players pulled some shenanigans when the ump wasn't looking their way. For instance, a runner might cheat by running directly from first to third base, or by cutting the corner at second base without touching the bag.

Fielders cheated too. On a long hit to the outfield, the runner might be tripped as he rounded first, bumped when he passed second, and have his belt held when he reached third. First baseman Adrian "Cap" Anson, who was the

BP: batting practice

dingers:

home runs

high heat:

a fastball

gas: a good fastball

Uncle Charlie:

a curveball

captain of the Chicago team, had his belt loops replaced with a long belt "tube." Why did he do this? Because when he was a base runner, it was more difficult for fielders to hold on to his belt to slow him down!

Cheating didn't stop with holding on to a runner or cutting across the diamond. Some teams would freeze baseballs, which made them harder to hit far. A few decades ago, Denver's team did just the opposite with their batting practice balls—they heated them to make them go farther. The visiting teams looked

RAINBOW

HEATER; HIGH HEAT

DEUCE

GAS

UNCLE CHARLIE

on in awe as the Denver batters took **BP** and hit nothing but **dingers** with the warm baseballs!

One kind of cheating that has always been allowed is sign stealing, where a player or coach can see what sign the catcher is giving the pitcher and then signal to the batter that it is going to be **high heat**, **gas**, or **Uncle Charlie**. Sometimes it is the coach at third base who can see the catcher signaling for a **rainbow**, a **deuce**, or a **heater**. Other times it is the runner on second base

rainbow: a sweeping curveball

deuce: a curveball, usually signaled by the catcher by putting down two fingers

heater: a fastball

31

twinbill: also called a doubleheader. Two games played between the same teams in one day.

who sees the sign and signals the batter. This is not against the rules.

But here's a sign-stealing scheme that was against the rules: In 1951 the New York Giants had someone in the center-field stands read the signs through a pair of binoculars and then signal the pitches that were coming.

Or how about this one? In 1900 the Philadelphia Phillies tried a scheme that was discovered by a Cincinnati Reds third-base coach during a **twinbill**. He found an underground wire in the coaching box that led across the outfield to the Phillies locker room! There, a reserve catcher read the signs and relayed them to the Phils' third-base coach by a buzzer hidden in the dirt. The coach then signaled the batter what was coming. Something must have worked, because the Phillies won both games. The Phillies' owner ignored the newspaper accounts and charges of spying, but he did remove the wire.

Pitching Changes

For a few decades of the nineteenth century, most teams used only one or two pitchers for a whole season. Their **hoses** must have ached like crazy! Believe it or not, at one time batters could order

hoses: pitcher's arms

meatball:
an easy pitch to hit

gopher ball: a pitch
that will "go fer" a home run

lollipop: a slow pitch
that is easy to hit

glass arms:
pitchers' sore arms

free pass: a walk

Annie Oakleys:
walks. Named after a star of
the rodeo in the nineteenth
century. An Annie Oakley
was a free pass to the theater.

the kind of pitch they wanted, either high or low. Imagine telling a pitcher, "I'll have a **meatball**, and while you're at it, add a **gopher ball**, and I'll finish with a **lollipop**." Despite possibly having **glass arms**, those early moundsmen had a few advantages over today's pitchers. From 1876 to 1879 it took nine balls for a **free pass**, so **Annie Oakleys** were rare. The number of balls needed for a walk was gradually reduced over the next few years. The **hurlers** pitched in a box, the front of which was just forty-five feet away from home, instead of standing on a rubber that is sixty feet, six inches away as they do today. Even though there hasn't been a pitching box since 1892, writers still say that when a pitcher has been **lit up** and the manager **gives him the hook**, he has been **knocked out of the box**.

Back then pitchers used only one or two balls for an entire game, compared to the more than one hundred balls used in a major league game today. If the batter hit a foul ball into the crowds, the fans had to throw it back. It wasn't until 1916 that

Chicago Cubs owner Charles Weeghman changed the practice. "Oh, just let the fans keep the balls," he said, and within a decade the rest of the owners followed his lead.

hurlers: pitchers

lit up: when a pitcher gives up lots of hits

gives him the hook: takes a pitcher out of the game

knocked out of the box: when a pitcher leaves the game after giving up a large number of hits

doctoring balls:

altering balls by cutting, nicking, or applying some substance

NYAA NYAA!

Why would it be better for the fielding team to use fewer balls per game? Here's why: Balls that are used for a while soften up and don't travel as far as new balls when they are hit. Used balls are darker and dirtier, making them harder to see than a new, clean, white ball. Until it was outlawed in 1920, pitchers were allowed to spit on the balls, or put pine tar or petroleum jelly on them—anything to make them react in a funny way when thrown. One pitcher even licked the baseball while the other team watched. *Yuck!* They got back at him by putting hot sauce on the ball. By the third inning, his tongue was numb!

Even after **doctoring balls** was outlawed, pitchers continued to try to get away with it. Hall of Famer Gaylord Perry (who pitched for eight teams in his career) was accused for years of using petroleum jelly to grease the balls. He would even psych out opposing players before games by loading his hand with petroleum jelly and talcum powder and then shaking hands with the other team's sluggers. These players were then convinced that he was throwing balls loaded with gooey stuff, even when he wasn't. After he retired, Perry approached a petroleum jelly manufactuer about endorsing their product. He was reportedly turned down with a one-line postcard that read, "We soothe babies' backsides, not baseballs."

Pitchers would often doctor a baseball by scuffing it or nicking the stitches with a sharpened belt buckle. This would allow the pitcher to make the ball curve more. In 1987

Phillies pitcher Kevin Gross got thrown out of a game when umpires found sandpaper in his glove while he was pitching against the Cubs. He was suspended for ten games—he didn't get his glove back until August 1991! In 1980 Seattle Mariners pitcher Rick Honeycutt taped a thumbtack to his finger to cut the ball. Unfortunately for Honeycutt, an opposing player spotted the tack from second base. When the umpires found it, they **thumbed** the pitcher **out of the game**.

thumbed out of the game:
to be ejected from the game

Batter Up!

Batters, like pitchers, want to get an edge. Sometimes they hollow out a little bit at the end of the bat. But some players try to doctor or cork their bats by cutting off the ends and hollowing out the hitting area of the bat. Then they jam in cut-up rubber balls or cork and glue the wood end back on. This makes the bat lighter to swing, and players feel they can hit the ball farther. In 2003 slugger Sammy Sosa of the Chicago Cubs was caught using a doctored bat in a game when the bat broke in half and the cork spilled out. He claimed he just used the bat for batting practice and didn't mean to use it in a game!

tater: a home run

Decades ago, hitting a **tater** over the fence was close to impossible with a doctored-up ball. Making things worse for batters, many ball fields were much larger than modern fields. Most home runs were

alleys: areas of the outfield that are between the outfielders

hit in the **alleys** and were inside-the-park homers. In other parks, like Chicago's tiny Lake Front Park, where Chicago's National League team played, the outfield fence was so close that balls hit over it were ruled doubles. Lake Front Park's left-field fence was just 180 feet out! It's no wonder that in 1884, when the doubles rule was changed just for the season, Chicago hit 131 of their 142 home runs at home. Also in that season, Ned Williamson hit 27 home runs—25 at home—to set a home run record that wasn't broken for thirty-five years. The next year they changed the rule back and Williamson hit just 2 homers at home. And do you know who broke the record in 1919? Babe Ruth, with 29 homers. He was also 9–5 on the **hill** that year.

hill: another name for the pitcher's mound

Trading Places

By the way, selling and trading players has always taken place and has always been booed or cheered by fans. But if you think players have been traded only for money, here's some food for thought: Chattanooga shortstop Johnny Jones was traded to Charlotte for turkeys so that the Chattanooga team could have a Thanksgiving dinner. Minor league pitcher Joe Martina was traded for a sack of oysters, and worst of all, Jack Fenton was traded to San Francisco of the Pacific Coast League for a bag of prunes.

portsider:

a left-handed pitcher

But the most famous sale in baseball history took place in 1919 when the Yankees paid Boston $125,000 for Babe Ruth. From 1914 to 1919 the Babe had been a pitcher for the Red Sox, all the while playing outfield when he wasn't pitching. At the time, he was the best **portsider** in baseball *and* the most feared

44

slugger! He also got lucky: A new rule outlawed the practice of spitting on and doctoring balls. Now the balls were cleaner and easier for a batter to see, and the Babe went **deep** 54 times. The next year he **went downtown** 59 times; the runner-up hit only 24 home runs! It wasn't that they were **Punch and Judy hitters**—back then, the style of play tended toward hitting singles and doubles. At least until the Babe came along. In 1930 the Babe was pulling in a salary of $80,000—that's about $800,000 in today's dollars. When asked why he deserved to make more money than the president of the United States, he replied, "I had a better year."

deep: Going deep is hitting a home run.

went downtown: hit a home run

Punch and Judy hitter: a player who just slaps singles. Not a home run threat.

YES, BASEBALL WAS DIFFERENT BACK THEN, WITH DIFFERENT RULES, STARS, PLAYING FIELDS, AND EQUIPMENT.

But the game's past is connected to the present, and baseball has a longer history and more records than any other sport does. Legend has it that the game was invented by Abner Doubleday in 1839 in Cooperstown, New York. That's just a tall tale. Baseball evolved from simple European bat-and-ball games played in the eighteenth and nineteenth centuries. But baseball quickly gained popularity in the United States. Even before the Civil War, in the 1850s, baseball was referred to as "America's Game." That was forty years before basketball was invented!

Today baseball is referred to as the "National Pastime." Even casual fans know the names of earlier

the show:
the major leagues

stars and some of the more famous records: Joe DiMaggio's 56-game hitting streak, Ted Williams's .407 batting average in 1941, Barry Bonds's 73 homers in 2001, or Cy Young's 511 career wins. Yankees and Mets manager Casey Stengel once said, "You can watch a game every day and see something you have never seen before." This is still true today—and it will be true one hundred years from now.

Yet you have to wonder how **the show** will change in the next century. Of course the game will evolve and new stars will always come around to break

Barry Bonds's or Babe Ruth's records. Maybe the equipment and playing fields will change too. But there's one thing you can count on: Batters and pitchers will always glare at each other, sluggers will always hit home runs, and umpires will always thumb out managers who argue too long. And each team will always try to find new ways to win!

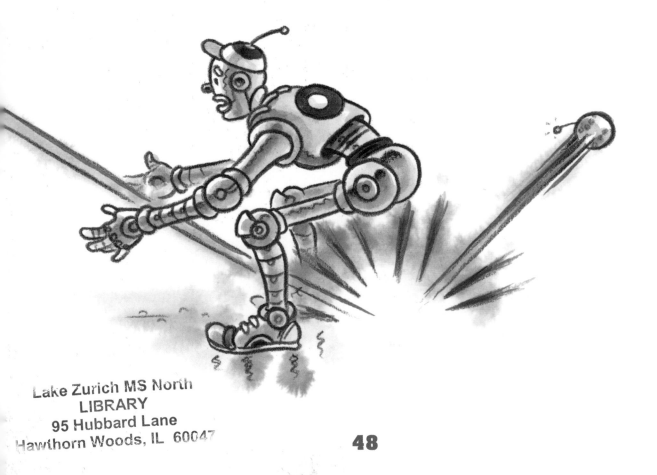